P9-DGL-888

Sending Messages with Light and Sound

by Jennifer Boothroyd

first step nonfiction

Lerner Publications · Minneapolis

LERNER

SOURCE™

Expand learning beyond the printed book. Download free, complementary educational resources for this book from our website, www.lernerresource.com.

Copyright © 2015 by Lerner Publishing Group, Inc.

All rights reserved. International copyright secured. No part of this book may be reproduced, stored in a retrieval system, or transmitted in any form or by any means—electronic, mechanical, photocopying, recording, or otherwise—without the prior written permission of Lerner Publishing Group, Inc., except for the inclusion of brief quotations in an acknowledged review.

The images in this book are used with the permission of: © Paul Prescott/Shutterstock.com, p. 4; © racorn/Shutterstock.com, p. 5; © iStockphoto.com/kozmoat98, p. 6; © Alexander Helin/iStock/Thinkstock, p. 7; © Oleskii Sagitov/iStock/Thinkstock, p. 8; © motodan/Shutterstock.com, p. 9; © iStockphoto.com/travismanley, p. 10; © Hemera Technologies/Ablestock.com/Thinkstock, p. 11; © Mimadeo/iStock/Thinkstock, p. 12; © giko/iStock/Thinkstock, p. 13; © iStockphoto.com/seanfboggs, p. 14; © Pressmaster/Shutterstock.com, p. 15; © Cottonfioc/iStock/Thinkstock, p. 16; © Michael Rolands/iStock/Thinkstock, p. 17; © iStockphoto.com/OJO_images, p. 18; © jvdwolf/iStock/Thinkstock, p. 19; © Sabina Salihbasic/iStock/Thinkstock, p. 20; © Jose Luis Pelaez Inc/Blend Images/Thinkstock, p. 21; © selimkskan/Collection/Thinkstock, p. 22.
Front Cover: © Belinda Pretorius/Shutterstock.com

Main body text set in ITC Avant Garde Gothic Std Medium 21/25.
Typeface provided by Adobe Systems.

Lerner Publications Company
A division of Lerner Publishing Group, Inc.
241 First Avenue North
Minneapolis, MN 55401 USA

For reading levels and more information, look up this title at www.lernerbooks.com.

The Cataloging-in-Publication Data for *Sending Messages with Light and Sound* is on file at the Library of Congress.

ISBN: 978-1-4677-3913-9 (LB)
ISBN: 978-1-4677-4687-8 (EB

LC record available at https://lccn.loc.gov/2013048313

Manufactured in the United States of America
7-44991-16076-11/3/2017

Table of Contents

What Are Messages?

Messages give us **information**.

We send messages over
a distance.

We learn from messages.

There are many ways to send messages.

Light and sound help us
send messages.

Sending Messages with Light

Big lights can send messages.

The elevator is going up.

So can small lights.

Traffic lights help drivers.

Lights can tell people where to go.

Lights can warn of danger.

Sending Messages with Sound

Loud sounds can send messages.

Quiet sounds send
messages too.

A clock's ring is a message.

An **alarm clock** rings.
It's time to get up!

Your words make a message.

We share news by talking.

We listen to the radio. We hear voices from far away.

Sirens make a loud noise.

Sirens warn people of danger.

Sending Messages with Light and Sound

Some messages use both light and sound.

These lights and sounds mean a train is coming.

A train crossing has ringing bells and flashing lights.

The lights and sounds on this fire truck tell people to move away.

Fire trucks have flashing lights. They have loud sirens too.

Cell phones use both light and sound.

People can hear and see messages on cell phones.

What messages can you send with light and sound?

Glossary

alarm clock – a clock that can make noise at a set time

information – details about a person, place, thing, or event

messages – information sent from place to place

sirens – machines that make a very loud and often high-pitched sound

Index